Holding on to Happiness

JOSHUA

Library of Congress Control Number: 2025913317

ISBN
978-1-964488-75-2 (Paperback)
978-1-964488-76-9 (eBook)
978-1-964488-74-5 (Hardcover)

Dedication

*This book is dedicated to my sister and my mother. Together, they brought
me to a different level. Specifically, a level where I could achieve all.
I used to think my publisher would be my "pull." While my family
would be my "push," Therefore, the dynamics of the two (my family and
my publisher) would be established while I was working on the book.
Almost as if representing an opposite-and-equal reaction repeated over
and over. That's how I'd essentially achieve results. "Going with the
flow" while, simultaneously, letting the push-and-pull lever move back
and forth, establishing a masterful compilation of "Happiness's" tenets.*

*My sister and my mother reside in the same city as I.
Specifically, in the corridors of the North Country, also
referred to as the "mecca" of New York State.*

TABLE OF CONTENTS

INTRODUCTION

I've embarked on a creative journey, birthing a collection of works, although I use the term "pieces"; reluctantly, for my publisher prefers it that way. These creations have allowed me to venture into uncharted territories, exploring profound themes such as "Energy"; and "Power." While the former delves into the world of facts and reality, the latter takes the shape of fiction, allowing me to wield the pen like a brush, painting narratives that navigate the intricate realms of human nature.

In these narratives, I strive to illuminate the ever-elusive pursuit of absolute happiness, a quest that often leads individuals to the boundaries of their own existence. To grasp the essence of these intricate human complexities, one must journey beyond the surface of conscious thought and delve into the collective and subconscious layers of the mind.

It's within these cerebral catacombs, amidst the labyrinthine corridors of memory and imagination, that our most profound contemplations unfold. Here, the inner workings of our minds are brought to life, like synchronized neurotransmitters firing in harmony, channeling positive thoughts and illuminating the path to our deepest desires.

As day turns to night and we slip into the enigmatic realm of REM sleep, our subconscious unfurls its wings, giving flight to dreams that are a testament to our deepest desires. These dreams flow like an unbridled river, much like those ephemeral moments of a "wet dream"; guiding us toward our most profound aspirations, all orchestrated by the commanding forces of the frontal cortex. In this symphony of the mind, neurotransmitters dance in rhythmic harmony, composing an intricate symphony of thoughts.

Amidst this intricate tapestry, there are neural axes that wield control over our cognition, guiding us towards an understanding of the world around us. This complex yet beautifully orchestrated symphony creates a structure that seems indestructible, much like the inexorable force of inertia. It's as if this innate drive clings to the very essence of inheritance, cradling it possessively, and nothing in its path can hope to shatter its resolve.

Like a river following its predetermined course, this force of inertia navigates through the labyrinth of existence, untouched by the obstacles that may seek to disrupt its journey. It nurtures the development of an unburdened, sheltered entity, ensuring that no external influence derails its path. This unwavering trajectory represents the essence of creative and aesthetic vitality, but it also serves as a guardian against potential disruptions, steering life toward an immutable destiny.

In the grand tapestry of existence, this unwavering journey represents the ideal element, steadfastly connected to the "essence of happiness". It's as if happiness itself were a magnetic force, inexorably drawing this intricate structure toward its ultimate realization.

So, I invite you to embark on a journey through my works, where the quest for happiness is an ever-present undercurrent, guiding our souls along a path illuminated by the beauty of human nature and the resolute force that drives us forward. Welcome to a realm where imagination and reality entwine, and the pursuit of happiness becomes the captivating heartbeat of our existence.

CHAPTER 1

"Happiness is a Warm Gun"

"Happiness is a warm gun." This was a song by the famous band The Beatles. Alright, maybe this is true. Is happiness ready to explode at any minute? Is happiness something that happens at a moment's notice? Let's think about it. John was raised by a single parent and it was his dad. One whom apparently couldn't provide the resources to excel according to happiness. He often wrote about how miserable he was.

John may have been wrong. I'd like to prove that happiness can be sustained.

I moved into an apartment recently. It fits the description of a worthy place to settle down. It consists of a kitchen, a bathroom, and a living room. It also includes a living area outside the complex. Now, what is it that a peaceful neighbor would ask for? It is the state, if not the condition, of being happy. In order for happiness to occur, there must be a condition for it to occur. That's in the moment!

When I moved into the place I was greeted by another neighbor. His name is Fred. When I loitered freely on property, was I disturbing the peace resembling this man– was he the property?

Being a peaceful guy, I showed him that he could have empathy for the individual I was. I communicated with him in a nonverbal way. Frank takes local trips to Saranac Lake occasionally. He must be doing this in order to breathe in the fresh air of Saranac Lake. Therefore, he's not property.

Frankly speaking, that was the first encounter. What I learned was that you don't need to communicate happiness. Happiness lies within the individual. Hell, the individual may be introverted or extraverted. The main thing one has to understand is that it lies with the individual.

My second encounter was with a neighbor by the name of Debbie. We both expressed our happiness to start. Unfortunately, we'd learned that happiness couldn't be concealed. We engaged in intimate sex a couple of times. The truth being seeking the individual and matching it, humbly with happiness. Thereby in that relationships of any kind would seek sustenance by the constraint of time. What is important to know is this type of activity, sex invokes only brief happiness. Moreover, in a Platonic role. Furthermore, not in a carnal one. However, if you can find a niche in the various styles, then one could sustain that feeling. Thereby, said and done; the limit to sex means a development in transcending positions. In other words, an empathetic growth towards oneness. Third, was my encounter with Dot. Dot is an elderly woman. She has a mild case of dementia. To be in tie with karma: for karma is a necessary means for survival in the moderate age where we tend to rely on collaboration. She enabled brief happiness due to me by not displaying stereotyping.

I don't know if she knows what happiness is. However, I do know she is a quality individual. She tends to be like a chameleon. She changes colors in a positive note. She is my neighbor, and I trust she will change like a chameleon does. What I mean by this is that I hope she finds happiness in any ordinary individual. That would be good.

What if there was a hospital, military, or government without beauracratic control? This would mean there would be a possibility to operate under one's own discipline. When I was in Boston, I belonged to a Tae Kwon Do group. It wouldn't be wise to bring up "control" to the instructor. Markie was a black belt at what he did. He would advise us to have control over our body movements. This is also the exact point of yoga and meditation. To have control is to exert self-exposure. When this is done, a person can experience happiness. To sustain it would mean setting limits not on what you do; however, on the people giving limits.

When I was in the military, the drill sergeant issued limits on how we performed. If they weren't followed one would have to suffer the consequences. This often involved doing pushups, sit-ups, or even a bear crawl which I experienced often.

However, one must realize limits can be surpassed by the individual. Often, there is someone who violates a given limit. After this occurs, there is loss of control. Furthermore, there is this loss of happiness. How can it be sustained then?

I was at the hospital today. What happened was I was sent into this room. People all over were complaining how they were either hurt, violated, or being at the wrong place at the wrong time. From what perspective does one wind up in such a predicament where their self-limits were surpassed?

Being an introvert has helped me to see that my own limits can only go partially sound in such ways. It is selfish to assume I can do anything! What advantage does this have? I mention discipline because people such as the Stoics used it to ultimately produce happiness in a structural society.

Freedom is not a word. Its understanding you can move in any direction at any given time. Yes, this may appeal to the reader. Moving in any direction deemed desirable leads the person to believe he or she has control. When this occurs, naturally, the person has control over his or her happiness. Now, I can go for a walk, shoot pool, or I could flirt with women. This all would involve me moving in a certain direction. Holding on to happiness is the first step. It may take baby steps. Taking that first step-that is what takes courage.

There was a time in my life when I couldn't move in that free direction. Why was that? This goes back to beau acratic control. Seeing that you have it means you've got it. Only then can it be followed and maintained.

I have had recent encounters with the female. She has taught me that giving my input helps a relationship to function. Why? Debbie was shy at first. After giving her time, she opened up. This is when it happened! I learned that by being I presented an opportunity for ample freedom.

Love offers limitless boundaries that even the government, military, or hospitals fail to address. This is when that baby step is necessary. Take it at will, take it with helping hands, or take it seriously! What does this mean specifically? It means as once stated, "Love is the food of music" (Shakespeare, W). To supplement by saying (in a development leading to a committed, trusting, and understanding marriage), love triggers a medium to become that leaf. A resulting leaf that has magically budded off its own branch: a branch representing ones "actuality-potential" (as pointed out by Aristotle).

Debbie did this. She used her will in determining our happiness. It may have lacked love of any sort. What she did (no strings attached) essentially by opening up was sharing her happiness she had. However, lacking platonic or carnal in a sense. Instead, committing to sharing, and caring for a development of the mind. In depth, a rewiring of the brain due to the expansion of neural transmitters resulting from euphoric activities. Ones that include physical, mental, and emotional capacities that are essentially attained from a mere fission/fusion from establishing a consolidated union (as evidently seen with mitotic/meiotic cell expansion). I had had other encounters with the "third kind" but in a loving sense. There was Emily, Jayme, Anna, and many others.

These experiences taught me I can hold on to happiness because it's possible.

Having said all this I can assuredly assert that women hold happiness, from time to time, by themselves. I find that absolutely fine! Who wouldn't want a wo man asserting their own control? In other words, aren't men and women striking upon this intercession state stemming from a shared autonomy in a sense? Dorothy showed this for sure. She demonstrated how she could strike upon this incessant state. Overall, a yearning endeavor for control (this involving the natural trend towards setting limits for other people-and in sense of seeking the programmed drive to surpassing it) carefully touching on mediocrity. AN overall balance according to the pre-programmed system (self-creating, self-sustaining awareness).

What if we just saw happiness neither as a warm gun nor as a moment? If happiness were sustained nobody would have to worry about utilizing their efforts in work, play, or bonding.

In a moment of time, you are there but you cannot see anything. This is where the world stops. This is when it is safe to say- it's time to call it quits. No, you cannot have this notion. Relatively speaking or absolutely, a person cannot ever get this idea.

We're just atoms and atoms tend to collide. Here, is where you can say, yes. It's time to step outside the veil. It's time to show your true colors. Isn't that what happiness is?

I have found happiness with an immense amount of people. There's Sofia, "Peff", Mishia, TJ, Bob. That's only to name a few. Happiness occurs when one least expects it because it is such a wonderful state of mind. Heck., one could expect it positively. On the opposite end of the spectrum, one could deny its existence and live in accordance to fear, uncertainty, and boredom. Happiness cannot be contained. Why is this so? Happiness is a phenomenon that needs to be released. As Barbie, my assistant for WRAP showed us if a feeling is contained within a container, it will inevitably explode.

I've had many experiences where this has occurred. One in particular was with my friend "Peff". I remember it was a very cool, brisk day. I was a good day for hiking. We were driving down the interstate listening to some music. What's the saying go, "love is the food of music"; so, play on". On the way, we shared feelings with each other. However, when we got there, I had an inexpressible emotion. It wasn't anger. It was sadness. It was happiness. I needed to reveal this. Thus, I spontaneously jumped out of the vehicle and started running to the base of the trail.

It was like no other ordinary feeling I've ever had. "Peff" and I experienced a lot of those feelings together. Delving in those emotions has kept our friendship intact. Most importantly it had driven us to the top like climbing mountains and reaching their apexes.

Reaching the apexes of mountains is one way of preserving happiness. Lord knows, I've been to a lot of apexes of mountains. "Peff" and I used to share these feelings of happiness. Reaching the top of a mountain enables "you" to freely go on with this feeling. I don't know if it is the beauty one see's or if it is the feeling of climbing a mountain one receives.

There have been three mountains I've enjoyed climbing. One is Rattlesnake. This lies just south of Willsboro. Willsboro being a point of reference because it lies in a defined, easy to get to range. However; this is not any ordinary range but a subsidiary one. By this one tends to think it may be a hill! No, it's a mountain. Nevertheless; it's a mountain of God's creation-nothing more!

Willsboro is a town situated in the niche of Lake Champlain. It's a pleasant climb for the most part. One experience was by me. I was in the process of climbing and I had a realization that time had stopped for me. What existed were nature and the breeze that only gave me inspiration to continue climbing. I think it was that time I crossed paths with two others. I cannot remember their names. They gave me directions to the top. So I continued the climb and reached the top.

There was another time; I climbed Rattlesnake with my dog. We didn't quite make it to the top. What happened was we arrived at some part of the trial that looked brutally wiped out by loggers. I said to myself," I've never seen this before." The dog agreed and we turned around. We still enjoyed the hike back. In fact, I raced the dog on the way back.

That's just it. Happiness will enter the mind. It will sneak up on a person especially when that person is doing such an activity as hiking. The best call is to seize that chance of having it enter the brain. Cause it to continue by furthering the process that allowed it to enter the brain.

Another mountain I climbed was called Pocomoonshine. This mountain is located adjacent to a body of water. My thoughts are that no one utilizes this source. It's a mountain that brings harmony to the soul.

I remember one time I came from work. I had a mind of emptiness one will experience after meditating. Of course, I opened Pandora's Box and explored the emptiness. What occurred to me during this was that I had love, support, and guidance from others. This brought me to the realization that I was happy.

So, I have continued to climb mountains. At times, I've climbed them with my dog and other times by myself. As I explained, I'm an introvert. I seek within for a sense of self. This is similar to the Eastern religions. However, I'm not a man of Eastern dogma. I'm Unitarian. Given at alms to create and never destroy. Why not strive at this impetus. Destroying involves all the doors of building a life. For example, one like myself would not inevitably get married, have kids, nor have a home. In this case, for the matter, is good to benchmark this principal of object permanence (the "idea": objects not seen in reality still exist; furthermore, they can be created or destroyed-moving forward, and doesn't this equivalate with happiness?) The opposing perception must be demanded. For it is at this junction, in and of itself, true life gets delved, and by being one brings all sorts of happiness.

I've also climbed a mountain by the name of Hurricane. From time to time, I've attempted to reach this place. I've driven down roads. These roads have often lead me astray. It truly is beautiful in Keene Valley.

Hurricane Mountain lies nestled in the "valley". It is a longer hike. It takes more energy to scale. The most exciting part of it is that it winds around. Take the trailhead and it leads you through bogs and extremely beautiful nature. Furthermore, there are paths that consist of bridges. These bridges are constructed from the people that care for the mountain.

One time I scaled the mountain I was with a friend. There are sudden but brief slants we must climb. These are fun. They definitely give us happiness. What happens is we unexpectedly reach plateaus that make it difficult on our minds. We think to ourselves, there is going to be another brief slant we're going to have to climb. Most importantly, this is the process.

The top is momentarily reached and is breathtaking. Like every mountain in the range there are rocks one can sit on. It is during this period where happiness is sustained. An observer may enjoy the scenery. An actor may recklessly jump off the rocks onto other rocks. Its important to know, we pushed ourselves mainly to maintain. IT's by these practical approaches to living collectively with others with similar drives. This is where one becomes full of awareness. One, recognizes, by oneself, energy can essentially be conserved-what else (Shultz, Modern Psychology)? We've together reached this pinnacle. All these culminating dynamics exploding into momentary bursts of happiness. Furthermore, its by understanding these motivating, self-esteem producing processes. In other words, a forward analyzation enabled by a sense of introspection which empowers, validates, and connects an individual with the interacting environment.

I've also climbed Hurricane with my dog. My dog is very receptive to happiness. He often is at my legs imploring for more. Anyways, we take on the hike together. We approach various trail markers with relief. It's demanding on our bodies. Knowing that this awesome emotion exists frees the mind and opens us to the creator.

Charlie and I make stops. Besides the relief at the trail markers-we'll stop and play at water niches. We absolutely love the water. How exciting to splash water on ourselves. It takes some audacity for the first dip but we go through with it. Often, we do it with open hearts.

Relationships can be impossible at times. They do have their flaw's as setting control does. What seems most plausible to me is that they tend to give off an unsatiating inertia. This belongs to happiness.

I've been with a few during my lifetime. They are quite amazing in that they provide a chance to experience happiness. However, it's not the same as maybe experiencing "it" on a mountain peak.

Claire was a person with uncertain attributes. They were seen to come from her mom and her sister. She potentially offered a means to get away from the everyday life. She was a kind and loving female. She had qualities that attracted me to her. Believing I could pass the test, I attempted to have sex with her. Unfortunately, it didn't work.

Time slowly passed. I was unsure if we could even have a relationship. Truthfully, my mother pushed it once. I ultimately tried to surpass the boundary with her. Now, I'm a bachelor so it is easy to say that. It didn't occur to me that Claire was a person who needed affection like I did. Fortunately, we did discover a means to connecting on a level that brought happiness.

There were many times we would spend time together. One time that just pushes the letter through the envelope is when we played tennis together. She was good. So was I. Tennis gave both of us an outlet to perform to our personal levels. We exerted ourselves to the extremes. It is safe to say we accomplished it. What we found was that by focusing on a sport, we could transmit our energy into each other. So we played often. Whatever the weather turned out to be, we managed to play. I remember one time it was raining hard. Nobody was out on the courts. What I did was foolishly try to show my manhood to God.

It was foolish and immature. I realized this but something else was driving me to do this. The Lord didn't communicate back. I wasn't struck by lightning or the storm didn't stop. I stopped playing tennis and so did the others.

What I struggle to recognize is that by using this energy to validate our happiness meant. It didn't exactly mean the world to us but close to. Seeking pleasure from activities is what we both wanted. We strove to finish the day and carry them out.

This is when we found the limits to happiness. We would frequently go from one activity to another. I'm sorry to say, but happiness has its limits. Although, I may seem hypocritical- it's the truth.

The other person I had an opportunity to share with was Desire. Desire came from a family with caring parents. They provided her with a chance to grow as a person.

We met at a fraternity/sorority gathering. I was with a friend, and she was all alone. What happened was that we got to discuss our lives while enjoying the fun. Was this happiness or was it something else. Was it love? I beg to differ. It only lasted roughly a month. She was fond of me and I was fond of her.

What we didn't realize is that while we were together, we were happy. Whether it was being away from the family life, whether it was being away from the school life, or whether it was being away from reality.

Being united showed us that happiness could be reached. It was unique though. We were able to surely express our individualities. She was a person of an honest and loving character. I was a person unsure of myself. It turned out that we diverged. We essentially had gone on our own paths.

Now, let's look in retrospect at what John Lennon had to say. Let's look in retrospect at what Will Smith had to say. Surely, they knew happiness was realistically possible. Surely, they knew happiness was realistically plausible. What if happiness could be sustained by everyone? What if one could find no limits?

John and Will Smith both believed that happiness was momentary. Should it also be considered that this is the way and only way it can pervade one's consciousness? Is happiness for the greatest amount of people only necessary via momentary spurts?

Being a person having intellectual capacities causes me to wonder-really wonder. Is it happiness one ardently pursues? No. Is it happiness one freely has to prevent having been addressed of its limits? Happiness is a means to establishing oneness with oneself. It involves courage above and beyond to attain it and when it is attained there isn't a single problem.

I was about to enjoy Memorial Day and what happened? Debbie was waiting outside. I had to say "hi", so I did at least to it. The creator has granted us with certain qualities that cannot be abused. One of them is of friendship. Under Catholic dogma thou cannot covet thy neighbor. This being apparent and obvious! All around adultery is a "known" sin. Frankly, I didn't know and I didn't care. From a benchmark does one inevitably search for more? No, thats greedy.

Is this greedy endeavor? No, it is defined as will for a way. Waited and regulated in New York is explained in a validated discovery of human doubt. One cannot be certain with the exchange of listening did we move forward or did we move backward. Moreover; this form of "stinking thinking" and allows for doubt to overcome happiness. In this example, Dorothie is the point of reference which happens to evoke a sense of shared doubt. Shall it be? Would it be purpose to allow a woman, distraught from all previous conversation transfer it being doubt? Let's review: doubt represents an off or inexplicable feeling, emotion that arises out of uncertain purpose. Now, for an example: a tortoise is claimed to be slower than a hare. In and of itself, no way could the rabbit retain a slower speed. No way could a tortoise retain a faster speed. Thus; it rests on the parables doubt that existent was "stinking thinking" In validating any connectedness which would lead to happiness.

Religion done, is religion said. What this means is that any religion practiced must be complied to. If one was going to practice Islam, one would practice Islam. If one were to practice Christianity, one would practice Christianity. Finally, if one were going to practice Judaism, one would practice Judaism.

Holding onto a faith is extremely simple. It's like holding on to happiness. It takes patience. God knows it can be attained, so why not sustained! Holding on to happiness is imperative to survival in today's economic conditions. It involves courage, charisma, and action.

I was going to write about marijuana; however, I'm going to connect religion and happiness instead. Since the beginning of man, religion has been an outlet-a way to get away from everyday life. It has been used as a tool. What most atheists and agnostics don't understand is that it can also be considered an aphrodisiac.

I've had quite a few experiences with religion. They have all given me happiness to some regard. They've opened me up to the world in a strange, yet promising light.

Damn, if people could realize the absolute, yet blissful wonder of religion maybe we'd take a step towards no war.

When I was in Boston, I had joined a group of growing Christians. They had been lead by a person seeking the truth in life. His name was Calvin.

Calvin was married to another Christian. In fact, this ladies' family was devout in all senses. Her father was a preacher, and her mother was a rare housewife. Both helped themselves and others to see the imperative benefits to being Christian.

I remember one time I was at a service with the family and Calvin. I happened to be standing next to the father. At this time, I was agnostic. This man watched the preacher with me. He observed my moves. He noticed I wasn't really involved in the service. So he would share the Hymnal and coax me to singing aloud. He was a great man.

Other times Calvin and I would discuss the facets of Christianity. I would compare it with Raja Yoga (a tentative

Religion). This was the religion I was into at the time. So Calvin and I would engage in these long discussions on how scripture in the Old Testament predicted events (miracles) in the New Testament. Calvin was a big history buff, and I was an avid scholar who was willing to sacrifice time to learn the doctrines of Christianity.

Calvin wasn't the only one I learned about Christianity with. There were two other close friends I kept in touch with. There had been a time I was with them outside the place I had worked. This was the day of reckoning so to speak. Christ, I wanted to see faith and believe it. After praying we went outside. Here, the two just stood. It was breezy. We held hands and witnessed the wonder of the day. It was quite extraordinary to them-to say the least. I would like to explain the experience. What happened was that I had an epiphany. Faith is something one must grasp uncertainly. It's like betting on a game.

Ironically, at the same time I was with a group of Brahma Kamaris. They took a different approach to faith.

Susan was the leader of the group. She had her own apartment where people would come to visit and meditate. She had pictures of the founder of the religion in her home. Occasionally, I'd come to learn and practice their faith. I'd go the place and mediate in a room. This was one of the two rooms I meditate in. Here, we were asked to relax for the most part. We had to let go of all thoughts and essentially zone off onto a picture on the wall. Sometimes there were other people would guide this process. We're asked to plainly sit down and breathe. It worked and this is what had drawn me in to this faith. This is what kept me from becoming a true Christian.

Was it by coincidence that I was learning both religions at the same time? It's difficult to say. However, I do know they kept me occupied.

Anyways, let's refrain from this talk for a moment. The gist of this book is on happiness and holding on to it. So, I ask myself how religion and happiness are connected. It's quite simple. Both are orientated around people. As I learned from multiple experiences is that when people connect on something as awesome as faith, happiness is evoked. How is it evoked? Well, it occurs naturally in this case. Usually, it just occurs spontaneously.

CHAPTER 2

The Comforting Joy of Pets

Now, what would happen if this uncertainty were changed into certainty? Hopefully, this is when happiness can be sustained. This is the point where there are no limits! Well, yes it can happen.

At the beginning of time, there was dinosaur. At the beginning of time, there was caveman. What would happen if at the beginning of time, there was a pet? It could be a dog, a cat, or even a monkey. Humans have always sought a pet for happiness.

Chewy was my most recent pet. Chewy is well rounded and has qualities even other dogs wish they had. Our family bought chewy from a pet store. Yes, Chewy was bred and raised by his mother.

Chewy brought hope to our family. When he was bought he became my dog. Knowing that he was there for me brought happiness. It wasn't easy at first. The dog had to get used to living with humans.

In my high school days, Chewy did bring hope. Furthermore, he brought happiness in the most loving sense. I remember how I invited friends over to the house. Let's say they weren't of the best influence. They would often convince me to do drugs with them. In retrospect, I was also preparing to enter college. My grades were low and I wasn't the best boyfriend.

Chewy was there. Chewy always left a surprise for us. May it be excrement or just a toy? He was happy to reveal it to our eyes! If chewy was a bigger dog I wouldn't find happiness in him. There is something about the nature of this dog. He's cute… He's playful. Most importantly, he's there for you no matter what the situation.

When I was younger, I often became bored. It wasn't hard to be bored as an adolescent. Thus, I'd buy stuff for him. It could be a stuffed animal or it could be some other playful matter. I come home from school tired. I had to stay up! So, I'd find Chewy, and we'd play with his toy. It doesn't matter how small he was. We enjoyed playing. It is during this playing where happiness existed. If; the playing continued so did the happiness.

Charlie was my first pet. He was a lapsa-apsa. This was a rare dog. He had an enormous tail and was grey. This "dog" may have been abused but it kept a manner distinct and defining that displayed its personality.

I remember how we would take long trips with Charlie. Particularly, on this one trip the family-aunt included- were travelling from Idaho to Wisconsin. Of course, we had to take the dog for walks. This one time, we let the dog out. He wasn't leased. To our surprise it flew from the vehicle and almost got hit by a semi-truck. My aunt was surprised. My brother and sister were surprised! Is it the saying that cats have nine lives? Well, dogs have nine lives as well. Charlie survived and so did the aura of happiness for the family.

Charlie also used to honk the horn. The family and I would leave the car and go into an eating establishment. Trapper didn't like this. What would he do? He'd honk the horn! Unbelievable, I'd say.

For that instant, there was happiness. Again, that happiness evoked could have been prolonged. Giving the opportunity to incessantly honk the horn, would have brought that happiness.

So, time had passed. The interval between Charlie and the next pet seemed an eternity! Territory had to be expanded to the realm of the rodent. Thus, my parents had bought me gerbils for Christmas that year. Harry and Snowball were there names. Does one admit that there is pain in game? With

Harry and Snowball this very quotation sounds quite right. They bit and when they did they meant it.

As with any pet, these two creatures brought happiness. However, it was not in the way they looked but by the games I'd play with them. Snowball was white. Harry was grey. They were quick! Back in the day of raging adolescent sagas, Snowball and Harry had entered my world.

Often, I'd invite friends over to see the rodents. During these times, we spent a lot of effort caring for them. The sustained happiness followed in return. Happiness came from letting them out of their cages and trying to find them. As they were quick, they frequently got lost.

My friend and I had gone through this excitement one day. We let them out of the "cage" and let them run around freely. My friend got antsy so he tried to pick one up. Unfortunately, he suffered the consequences.

"Ow!" Craig said. He then subsequently threw the gerbil against the wall. "Ha, ha" I laughed. That was truly remarkable and exciting to see a friend getting bit by a smaller specimen. "Ha, ha"-I had to laugh. I couldn't quite but see such a hilarious event.

Yes, Harry and Snowball did die. When they were alive, having them in our presence was sheer happiness. Moreover, it was prolonged when the games didn't end. These were the games of hide and seek. As mentioned before, they bite too.

On a winter night when all was bleak, came along a cat whose name was Leo. Leo was different from any other pet. Leo was all around. Not like an all around athlete who could do the triathlon, but an all-around cat.

Seeking happiness from this entity required a heart for adventure. For, days to come the cat did die from just getting into this very adventure. It was killed by neighborhood dogs. To make a long story straight, Leo would do all sorts of things. Why, he'd lay across my shoulders. He'd hang from the rafters. He'd even lie in boxes.

How sweet a cat! People everywhere seek out happiness in its blissful state wondering will it stay. I concur but enjoy moments of peace as well. Sometimes-ironically-peace comes from in and of itself. Maybe the pet instructors preach upon focusing love, care, and all other energies on the pet. Then, maybe the focus can be considered 2nd nature to happiness. Now is a welcoming time to share an example: This happens to be covered in the latter end of the story.

One, of guru-ness to preserving the entity of happiness must work and proceed off all lines of work. As mentioned before, when fear and depression are apparent then becomes junctures that are blocked. In other words, these emotions caused both the amygdala and temporal areas restrict happiness due to the bereft blocking. However; when this focus occurs and empowers individuals to new heights. It is this at this moment when the emotion of happiness transcends. Parallel to enjoying and sustaining that peace with mountains or, formerly, the pets that gave my friend quite a headache!

CHAPTER 3

Show me the money

Given the circumstances I'm satisfied now and am trying to convince the reader to follow my advice!

Now, money is source of happiness. Although, I try to be immaterial, money is the answer to a lot of things. It can be intimidating at times. What is sought to glorify the individual is not the material that can be bought with it but with the ultimate satisfaction on receives holding a bill in his or her hands.

God knows it lasts until you find no other means to fulfilling it. What do I mean? Well, take for instance. A man is walking down the streets. He has his hands in his pocket. What are you going to think? Surely you're going to think this man has money and he likes it!

When I was in Portland, I experienced the financial downfall typical of any individual during this Economic crisis. I spent and spent money as if I were a spendthrift. Although, I wasn't I continued to spend. The happiness from money meant furthering my education. The purpose of my living in Portland was to go to Graduate School. If you were to look at a dollar bill, what would you see? Not the "Pursuit of Happiness" mind you. Instead, you see an honest American who also pursued a life in the vein of happiness.

I had a credit card. What this meant was that I had an obvious supply of money. Albeit, it came from a private company, I was bound to spend. So I did. There was much material to buy in Portland. Now, what I bought was items to place in my studio apartment. For I knew, I needed furniture, and I needed a medium to make me feel secure. Almost instantly after I moved in, I took a stroll to the store and bought a T.V. The best place to buy furniture was at a local thrift store.

Ultimately, one must strive for achievement. God willingly, this involves getting out from under the veil of poverty. Once you get there, you fall in love with materials. So, fortunately, I was attending Graduate School. In the long run, I'd be able to pay back my credit card debt.

I was able to buy the materials. So, I continued to go to school while buying more and more. It was a shame I spent so much. It leads to both financial and family hardships. Let the reader focus on the fact that buying items brought me to the realization that I had to earn money. Thus, I tried for a job in the area. Little did I know I was causing distress amongst my family?

My next encounter with money was after returning from Portland. I found myself back in Upstate New York. Money could only be used sparsely on my return. This was extremely hard. Fortunately, I had something to lean on. I had SSDI. SSDI stand for Social Security for people with Disabilities. This is a form of income coming from the government.

Happily, my first check amounted to nearly 17000 dollars. What was I going to do with all this money? This is where the story gets interesting. So, I received the money from the government. I was very much obliged. Money not earned but coming from such an important organization gave me assurance. It helped me to realize, yes, I do have security. Now, I had to budget the money. I began the process by going to my dad. He was the worthy yet stingy payee. He would be in charge of issuing the money to me after it was sent to the bank. This left me with less and less happiness. Fortunately, I knew money received would be money spent well. This, in turn, would bring me happiness.

Money is a material object, so as long as the machinery that produces it endures, so does the money. In order to sustain happiness with money the infrastructure that assembles money must be known. Golly, I reckon I can explain it!

First, resources such as oil and paper are supplied to produce the bills. Second, they are shipped to a factory where they are produced into the final product. Third, they are sent to the United States Treasury. Forth, it is distributed down the chain until it gets to the consumer. I hope that did it.

Gladly, money is now in the hands of the consumer or me. Luckily, I'm not the beholder of it! My father and I have set up a budget. It consists of paying off credit card debt, student loans, cell phone, and rent.

Now, I ask myself, "What else gives me happiness from having money?" It's all in the systematic process! Seeing money in my hands gives me happiness. Exchanging money for pleasure gives me happiness. Lastly, spending money on errands also gives me happiness.

The problem in all of this is that the money doesn't provide for lasting happiness. Then one would ask, "Why am I writing about this?" Well, it's simple. As an American we all have the rights to freedom. What would enable me to see this truth? I could go out now and spend it on food or other items. Heck, I could spend it on winning more money.

That's not going to happen! People have got to realize that! You have got to tell yourself happiness can be achieved and to do this involves the effort of making money. Pull it together and find a job.

Managing money is quite time consuming. Earning it may even be dire. I have a job! Absolutely, but why cannot you get job? "Well, it is because of the economy." Centering oneself on happiness requires an unfettered will power. It involves attention to what can be conceived as an individual desire.

On days of light, I'll motivate myself to walk somewhere to pay for amenities. These amenities must provide sustainability. In order, for me to survive me buys goods to sustain my happy feeling. Believing I have the drive, ability, and focus leads me to this short-term goal.

Eddie has done me good! He's been there for me. He's brought money back into my life. Assuredly, he likes money as I do. The point of the matter is we all strive for it. God, if we didn't, we would all be living a life unimaginable.

I don't understand how vampires like drinking blood. Today, I told a friend of Junior's that I like blood. That's just obscene. I would never drink blood from another person. It's funny how the world sometimes just lets go. People will operate like machines and let loose.

"Happiness is a warm gun" as The Beatles song goes. Yes, it could inevitably occur if precautions weren't taken. No, it isn't harmful. It cannot occur momentarily. It's all about intelligible being. Freely associating with that intelligible being means you can do anything, and God knows.

Momentary thoughts of happiness are blatantly stupid. They can only occur with proper work. See to it.

Holding onto happiness is similar to holding onto you. I know I'm not going to be famous. Heck, I even know I won't be rich. I do know that for the moment, I'll be thinking about the vast discipline I'll have when it comes to writing the rest of this book.

CHAPTER 4

A Preventing of Fear, Depression, and Doubt

The second half of this book is based on bringing about happiness. There are essentially three ways to do this. You can prevent feelings of depression. To do this involves delving into the mind. You can avoid situations that mean confronting fear. This can be an obstacle to achieving ultimate happiness. Finally, you can turn yourself away from the face of boredom by "acting". This involves having a plan. This involves having courage.

Depression has been a hallmark of individuals across the world. All cultures experience it. Admittedly, it takes a lot out of a person. When I was in college, I experienced it firsthand. I put myself in the confines of it! I wound up with the condition because I had lack of control. Yes, the environment does determine an individual's mind set. However, if happiness is within reach and sustained, then depression can be avoided.

I was twenty-one. God, I was at the legal drinking age. How wonderful it was to be 21 in America. I would often go to bars and ask for that beer that would take mind off the stresses of the day. Beer was and still is a substance that gives me momentary happiness. It instills a mood of "calmness" because it is an "anti-depressant". Of course, excess amounts can, ironically, lead to more depression.

So, I'd buy a beer and mingle with the crowd. I would get involved in pool games, talking, and flirtations. No one wants to admit all of this is a cause of the substance. I don't because I'm medicated and don't want to think, "Oh, I'm mentally incapable of engaging in these activities without the substance. It's a handicap. So, beer has and always will be a way to evade the conscious stresses of the day.

I also had frequent but unpleasurable trips to the casino while I was in Boston. I drop everything that had to be done and spend a day away from the apparent chaos of the city. It definitely has brought happiness to be away. The casino's environment offered luxury, which in turn brought happiness. The reader most likely will not read this part because gambling is a violation of a "good" happiness. Truthfully, when trapped within the confines of the city, you ought to be thinking "escape". Why? Only because "escape" presents a chance-and

I say chance- to free one's mind. This then brings s state of happiness that is prolonged with winning money.

To experience happiness in a different atmosphere also prevents the onset of depression. There is a novel chance to engage in activities that couldn't be engaged in at the other environment. You have to explore this chance! I was definitely left with this chance.

Fear is also a hindrance to happiness. Transference of this state occurs naturally when it isn't thought of. For this to occur, your won state must be seen through the eyes of your confrontation that evokes this "fear". Yes, it's natural to fear but when the other person's perspective radiates within, the happiness exists from knowing you are mainly connecting with it.

The only thing that a man cannot do is what he prevents himself from doing. I'm not saying women don't have this general weakness as well. Women have this but to a less extent. Since the beginning of "man", we've wanted to build, explore, and reproduce. It's all very natural. The truth is women, although it irrelevant, have been the recipient of whatever the man needs.

Fear is a reality because it exists in everyone's brain. This feeling occurs within the amygdale and is transmitted throughout the body (Baker, Dan, p.29, 2003). There are surely other parts of the brain responsible for fear (p.29). Through evolution, we as humans have developed a part of the brain known as the neo cortex (p.29). This is where intellect comes into play. If we could only reason, then fear would not be evoked!

Boredom was the last deterrent of happiness. Yes, boredom exists. The only positive way to alleviate or take it away is to act. This is when, God willingly; you can say you're happy. This is when you can say I have a life.

When I was a kid, I spent a lot of time doing activities by myself. I would shoot basketball, or I would throw a ball against the wall, or I'd go out for a pilgrimage, as you will, to my friends. All this was my part to be myself. I know this may sound like a contradictory concept seeing is that freedom happens outside the individual. Moreover, freedom is happiness.

Holding onto happiness requires a certain degree of level-headedness. Happiness consists of the fabric of a feeling. A feeling has no weight, in this case, as a feather. Float with the feather as a feeling floating in space!

When I was younger, I was apt to get into something foolish. Thus, I would do "daring" feats or I would smoke cigarettes, or I would smoke "pot". The fact of the matter is this riskiness helped me to be happy. I don't know if the "risk" gene is inherited. I do know it was provoked within.

Marijuana smoking eased the pain of thinking I'll be "number one jock", or I'll sit the highest on the bleachers, or I'll have the finest looking girlfriend. I didn't want these thoughts. I had a lot of significant plans. Ruining all plans would tell me I wasn't somebody.

It's funny. In retrospect, I did a lot. I took my friend's dares, I created fashion, and I fought hard to maintain an ideal image. I wasn't insecure nor did I have thoughts of being incapable. I liked myself. Sustaining happiness in high school meant the world to me. I don't know why.

I overtly reflect on those days of the past. I use those days as a tool to further my, God forsaken path now. I determine my fate instead of passively observing the world go round and round.

You can do this too. Let go of the premise that Happiness can be sustained. If you let destiny determine your outcome, you'll be waiting and waiting for that special day! Don't be passive. Behold the mightiness of not believing because believing is seeing.

Don't take life for granted. I took a trip today to SUNY Plattsburgh. It was a gorgeous day. I found myself going along the waterway. It was pleasant. The endless day took my worries away. I was feeling good. I made it. Being with happiness is all a part in growing. Moreover, growing takes away all seeps of sorrow!

Coming back from the realistic expression of fulfillment, I leaped across the log, and captured it. Frankly, I caught it while in mid air. Junior did offer me to help him with the groceries. I hesitated, due to the situation. So he caught it just like catching a butterfly in flight.

A hesitation is briefly uttered. No signs of life! No signs of Junior. He must have left to get some groceries. Anyways, I continued walking down the path and saw no means to getting across the river. However, there was a bridge. So I took the bridge. I reasoned that if I only was with someone else.

For the time being, I hesitated to follow my God given senses. I don't take much time though. I walk the remaining distance. I stop and take a look at the scenery. How serene. How beautiful. Down I go. My mental faculties are dormant for the moment. Frankly, I follow the path before me. Happiness is existent-it present because I want it to be. I lose all signs of peace and instead, fall into the abyss. It is dark down there. Forward in to the midst of cloudy decisions. Seek it though for it will bring riches.

Marijuana alters the conscience. Though, the substance can lead one to enter a clear state of mind. I'm not looking for this to get remarks from s business leader. No, I'm looking to convince the reader to look at the bright side. The person would only say, "It doesn't look so bright because the sun 'ain't' shining."

Marijuana is illicit and it will prevent you and the government from moving forward. Holding on to happiness takes a lot of courage. It may bring feelings down. It is important to realize, give it some time, and it will succeed.

There may be repercussions in finding the best suitable means. Take whatever comes your way. This is when it all comes together. Don't worry.

Don't go with your flow but go with your instincts. This is the way, because this is the way you were born. Don't just peddle with the flow of the city, but grasp it and throw it away. That's the power of your instincts.

Would you rest your head on a rolling log? I wouldn't. This definitely would be wrong because it's out of control. It will come. Now, that it has come, it is safe to say that marijuana is the choice of the person.

CHAPTER 5

Carpe Diem or, Carpe Mortem (Neglecting depression, fear, and doubt)

O.k. now it's time to get loose. You go with the flow. Take your shoes off. Walk on the floors. Take off from a passive-assertive, and flow with the flow. In his music, Eminem often urges listeners to drop their guard and fully immerse themselves in the here and now. When you do this, mindfulness naturally takes over.

Walk with a sense of purpose. Lose all sense of control. Let yourself go off into the world of illusions (imaginative). Commence flying; flying like antenna radio frequency and connect on "radio" waves. The sounds will permeate, pervade your skin. Nevertheless, as the ride continues let loose on one's emotion or emotions. Attachment exists but to a non-entity. The white noise and together angling, transmitting overtly on signal display. " Let nothing get you off a state of unconsciousness". This is precisely the appropriate time to transition back to reality.. That's when one is happy and, unconditionally when one is ready to return to reality. Nevertheless, we relatively cannot live in a world of REM-perhaps, were molded into a reality of conscientiousness. This enabling for appropriate decisions; nevertheless, consequential nature. In other words, intercession between reality and the imaginative. This is a part of living according to the instinctual drives, or the catalyst to drive us in to a self-perceived (as opposed to relatively made decisions and choices) world of making choices upon the reflected vise of reality. Transcendentally, we can learn after one realized what result are from previous consequences (otherwise known as rewarding behaviors). Transcendently, its by learning in which we experience freedom from being in an unconscious state of mind, body, and soul (pervading punishments preventing us from living the established co-existence of unconsciousness). This is where learning is unfortunately put to the side. Isn't it true we grow in terms of establishing a silver linings?

When I was in Boston, I took a trip to a religious facility. We had to remove our shoes! Then we had to follow orders.

Then we had to enter a room. We sat, we listened, and we meditated. It was this feeling-there. I froze and wouldn't let the self-go further. It won't happen. You've got to let yourself go. Free your mind of any obstruction that may enter. Have the aura of the atmosphere confine you senses. Place your bodily expression in the vault. Experience it firsthand.

That's when you begin to realize "Yes, I can do it!" Understanding you have reached this point means you can go further into the book. Ultimately you will render an able self. Now, open your eyes to the world that surrounds.

Reality finds its way back. Time to get out of it! Now, it's back to the sunshine and happy side of it. It's almost over. It's over. Sought was the state of "nothingness". This is Asian and it is followed by a lot of Americans out there. Delving into this state takes discipline, and it takes focus. It is art not science. Believing you have reached this, now, you're ready to continue.

Frank once told me to collect his bottles. I did. I was happy. Yearning for the vast multitude of pleasure involves courage. Having that courage only diverts one's attention to the fact that he can do it. Happiness collects all thoughts of wanting, needing, and desiring. It settles on only what you are thinking about.

Why doesn't the reader just coax him or herself to look inside? Eastern religion teaches this. In his film and music, Eminem repeatedly urges listeners to fully inhabit the present moment and never let a single chance slip by. This describes the essence of happiness. It takes heart and strife. In clarification, it takes courage to climb. As you move down an uncertain path, you may encounter abrupt obstacles. Focus all energy to reach that goal of happiness.

Mustering up the courage takes you to a higher level. "Halt." Devise a plan that you can drive down. It's up to you. Hold onto happiness and see for yourself. Sing yourself to that level of joy. Good, you're there. Now it is safe to say it is time for you to lean back.

Bringing yourself back out of the land of illusion requires a sudden switch from happiness. To do this means effort not on the beholder but on yourself. Don't relinquish this opportunity. Switching back and forth is a means to motivating oneself. Who's Joseph? Joseph is nothing but handwriting on a paper. I found the name printed in my neighbor's room the other day.

Joseph was both a carpenter and the father of Mormon religion. Was he happy? I'm sure the Joe who practiced polygamy was. Both found happiness in what they did. I think that if you find happiness in what you do your limits are limitless.

CHAPTER 6

Letting Go

When I was a student manager at Boston University I found that I could be inertia stricken when I reached a certain level. Specifically, when I had accomplished a job, I felt the entire world. Nobody likes the saying, "Life is a process." Well, I think that this is the means to an end. Just as reading may be a means to that end. Ironically, the end is "happiness" and since it's the end it has no limits.

So where do we go from here. Ultimately, I was thinking I could be more structured and continue to write about the sources. Instead, I'm just going to be free. Best said, is best done!

Methodologically, I carry out a routine based on the rewarded pleasures. I'll get up in the morning and go for a walk. I'll return and play the piano. Then I'll accept what the day has given me. I try not to depend on the weather because it is quite random. This methodological routine enables me to see myself. By seeing myself, I become happy. Is this true for work and experiencing of pleasures?

Of course routines have their negative side. One can become too absorbed in what they are doing; they fail to pay attention to what is going on around them. This may cause one to give into the bad-side (experiencing of self-inflicted punishments) and it may prevent you from not doing chores and not sticking to the routine during the day. Seize the moment as you were to seize the day. ITs by this methodology which brings convenient access to more rewards. Nevertheless, these so-called rewards can cause an extending period of happiness. Thereby, consciously avoiding punishing pain. A long time ago, when I was in my teens, I had to complete my homework every day. What I failed to do was let the words take me instead of me the taking the words. Due to this, I eventually found myself getting bad grades. I'd sit and not move forward. It drained me of all energy. I drained me of all ambition. Go with your inner drive and motivation. You know there's something down there.

Diving into a feeling is quite simple. It involves letting go. To do this doesn't come from any ordinary individual. It comes from an individual who understands him or herself. In the process of diving, try to focus on this very act. This is when a state of "nothingness" occurs. This would be affably supported by any Asian.

Music is something of a phenomenon. It expresses all beauty, all emotions, and all forces that exist. If we weren't to have music, we'd have nothing to fall back on. It is in the spirit of music where this state of "nothingness" occurs. How does it relate to happiness? Well, both are similar in that they allow for letting go.

In college I used to play the piano in a room. It was isolated from all other activities. TO make a long story short, I'd retreat into the room and let go. Although, I had a lot of studying to do and a life, I had to escape! SO, I did. Playing the piano offers solace and peace within the mind. It brings one to conclude, "Yes, I'm connected." I suggest you try to engage in such a leisure activity.

To understand people and how they attain happiness, one must delve into the sub consciousness. According to Freud, there are three levels of the mind. To know these levels means looking within. There are the superego, the ego, and the ID. The superego is primarily responsible for judgment of action. The Ego mediates between the superego and ID. The ID does nothing but hinder a person because it is responsible for instincts that are uncontrollable. This means if a person experiences happiness, then that person would be smoking weed all the time, or being promiscuous, or spending money excessively on gambling.

All this said, happiness comes when all three are working in a balance. All will be working in harmony. This usually occurs when there are no explicit influences. This occurs when there are no implicit influences. I'd have to admit, this usually occurs when operating with the "flow" In other words, letting oneself transcendently go.

Before, I began to write this, I had completed a work on Energy. Energy is similar in that it also operates with the flow. It's certain that forces cannot emit drive unless empowered to do so under inertia. Inertia is the free flow of anything. In space there are no influences. Thus, energy can act without influences. This is when it can be said that it's "going with the flow".

People at all levels see happiness as an entity. Why is this? Money is an entity. Or at least we perceive it as being an entity. O.k. so maybe happiness isn't an entity. Maybe it is just an intangible illusion. But, it does exist!

People can either act relative to what other people are doing or they can act absolutely by their own self-imposed will. Happiness finds its place with those who act in accordance to their own will. Why? It is by acting in accordance with their own will that they see they can control their feelings, emotions, and moods. People who act relatively only see what other people perceive happiness as being.

Looking back into the past, I've experienced both relative and absolute experiences. When I was in Boston and Student

Managing at the Student Union, I had to stay absolute. Orders were coming from me and if I were saying them indirectly, my subordinates would realize they were coming from someone else. That's not good. So, I'd direct people to their various tasks, and I'd happily let them complete each one at their own will. I couldn't tell if they were happy. I did know they were getting honest pay!

When I was in Portland, I wasn't doing the best. I kept to myself for the most part. I knew my journey to Portland wasn't going to succeed. Therefore, I depended on others. I lived in a relative vacuum. There was one specific time; my sister came out to visit. So, I planned ahead knowing I got happiness from other people. That was just it. I was incessantly living relative to other people's expectations. It may have been in school or on the streets. Anyways, I planted a lot of trees; whilst, I encountered a lot of bee's (when I didn't usually drink a lot)In the figurative form of being only left me bereft of energy because I wanted to be happy, but because I knew the people she hung out with drank. What were the consequences? Well, I wasn't feeling happy after the night ended.

While I was in high school, I have staunchly admit I was living absolutely. I had formed my own gang. I would swing on the swing while people gathered. My fashion defined me. All this played a part in me becoming a student at Boston University. Hell, I made it because I was myself.

I cannot think of another time I was living in a relative world. Maybe that's a positive thing. Choosing what world, you are going to live in depends on your faith God mainly because he has the power to choose it for you. Perhaps, it is a truth that some people determine their own fate.

I mentioned before that music has certain qualities to it. Well, yah, it does. Music is a catharsis in a way. It blocks out all negative thoughts. It lets in positive ones. Of course, someone may argue, well there is music that stimulates negative moods. No, all music is a gift from the soul. It carries with it a force that impels or compels someone to be happy.

So it is best that all people see music as an offering. Essentially, it is an offering to make a person worthy of all the riches in the world. Bob Marley, for example, urged listeners to free their minds from oppressive thought patterns—a call to mental liberation rather than literal bondage.

Give yourself an opportunity by releasing the tensions. Focus on a way to welcome happiness into your life. Build a pyramid in which happiness is centered at the pinnacle and spirals down into your life.

In the late 60's, happiness came to an abrupt halt due to the shootings of key political figures and the Vietnam War. America found a way to sustain this happiness. They found in such extreme ways as experimenting on drugs, having polygamous sex, and playing music to new heights.

All of this brought novel ideas to what our country really was about. Yes, we live on this land in pursuit of happiness. We strive at our occupations to earn this right to fulfilling it.

People like Bob Marley, John Lennon, and Arlo Guthrie exemplified the magnitude of how we could cope with the existing disasters. We could focus all happiness around each other like a circle of life. This would enable us to empower, connect, and validate each other.

CHAPTER 7

The Structure, The Function of Happiness

The 60's taught us a lot about ourselves. We could endure anything and change the body ruling us. Certainly, the government had its issues with the vanguard. Adapting to conditions maybe represented a catharsis to violence. The context: however, mimicked the presence of now. Amid a blatantly cry for revolution represented by Selma and Fergusson. Leaders such as WB Dubois and Martin Luther King Junior brought periods of brief happiness. They learned we weren't countries such as Stalin's Russia, Mao's China, or Hitler's Germany. We were a novel nation created out of God. This is a quote from Abraham Lincoln. We didn't get stuck in the "pit" so to speak-called Communism or Fascism. Instead, we climbed out of it by using our God given strengths and utilizing the framework of the Constitution of the United States.

Giving happiness to each other was the sole purpose for our existence as a country. It was mustered up through War, famine, and protest.

We all have flaws-yes that's certain- but we find ways out of them. I know, for instance, that I will smoke for quite a long time. I know I'm not going to be president. Fact of the matter is I'm not Jesus Christ. What I do know, however, is that this land is full of vast opportunities to live as a happy individual.

TJ is his name and checking out girls is his game. T.J. and I have been friends for quite a while. We have shared both up's and down's. We've tried to attain happiness together through multiple trips. We've gone to Canada on many occasions. Blaming him for no going anywhere is my fault. Given time, I'll get over my smoking and I'll get over what happened.

America is wide open. Frankly, I'd like the opportunity to see more of it! There are the beautiful countryside's. There are the gorgeous bodies of waters. There are the breathtaking landscapes.

Happiness is endless for far as I can see. If happiness were concealed to one area of this country, it would probably be California. Why? California offers a chance to grow with the flow. There might have been an energy crisis, but it's safe to say California is where the happiness is.

Writing this book has helped me to picture the future and what it entails. Being an American citizen most likely means I can be happy wherever and whenever. God, just show me the path and I'll present myself as one of willing and utterly knowing esteem.

Life is definitely a process. I discussed this half-heartedly with a friend of mine. Life requires knowing that "you can be all you can be". This is best said by the ARMY media. What I'm trying to say is that a person can look at it as a chance to move forward of move backward.

Systematically a person has the freedom to do either or. Now, I chose to move forward facing any obstacles that occur. Naturally, my problem now is striving to the top. I have confidence-God knows-but do I have the patience? No, that's the reason for writing this book.

Jokingly, if time could tell you what do, what would you do? Paradoxically, it tells you to stay put. If you were to move you'd be working with time.

Seeking a long career involves dedication and wit. It involves an aspiring yearning for success. Success only brings happiness. Success brings a sustained happiness!

When I was younger, I pursued athletics. Playing sports gave me the ability to be happily centered. It gave me strength to go beyond the limits. This is what you ultimately need to do. You need to go beyond the limits set forth by you and others. This will enable you to get a glance of happiness.

I played on many sports teams. They consisted of baseball, basketball, and soccer. With all the sports, I had the self-created goal to aim for the top. The process of doing this enabled me to see happiness in just that-the process. I excelled to captain on all teams eventually. I also lead a few teams to championships and claimed an All-Star spot in soccer.

The path ahead of me only construed of happiness. I would often dream of myself being a baseball great or shining in some other sport. You can do the same! Find something you have a passion for and just do it. Eventually, in the process you will lose all thoughts of anything else and truly experience happiness.

Leading my teams to victory, brought me more heart and care for what was to occur in my up-and-coming life. The challenges were there. The pressures were there. Most importantly, the love was evidently there. Now, the president faces a dire Economic condition similar to that of the Great Depression. What he has done is lead his country through the unhappy battle. He caused the nation to see him as charismatic. This, per se, has invited many to believe he is a special person with individualistic spirit.

Being an individual means climbing out of the shell of the family and reaching for a rope untouched by anybody else. It doesn't quite involve courage or "guts". It involves character and personality. If you stick out, the rope can be climbed!

Barak Obama had to live a life as an individual seeking identity. He had his parent and his grandparents to begin with. Subsequently, he had to strive for his own happiness on his own. He went to college obviously in Political Science. By expressing his character and personality he was accepted into Colombia. Here he was seen merely as "great". After college he became extremely rich as a business entrepreneur. Awe! What's the allure of being an individualistic business entrepreneur? Hell, I wanted to be one.

Barak was living happiness in itself. He was in the pursuit of happiness while simultaneously being happy. Now, you can see him today as President of the United States of America.

Lastly, I wanted to discuss the happiness one can have in a Sports team. It helps the reader to understand, yes, sports lead to happiness. However, that's not exactly what I'm going to share. What I'm going to share is about the happiness you can have in "rooting" for a team.

CONCLUSION

Yes, I'm through. Now, it's appropriate for the editing. Happiness evokes a person to think freely. Happiness has four sources mainly. They're mountains, relationships, religion, money, pets, and etc. Contradictory, there are three obstacles to happiness. They're boredom, fear, and depression. Overall, happiness can be utilized and sustained. This is done primarily by focus and inner drive. Holding on to it brings an individual to recognize his meaning. Presently I'm being asked to follow through with my uniquely self's happiness and fulfil a duty, better yet obligation to someone I truly do love. Specifically, I being asked to come out of my comfort zone and do a special favor. Planting a tree has not always been a favorite out of my "likings". Especially since I adopted this drear picture representing the modern environment. People who don't recycle have no clue what they are, presently, up against. A majority do, in awareness of climate change for the best. This will be my impetus, this soul recognition will keep me balanced in the face of that minority balance. Reaching out to this friend will relocate this feeling of attrition against the face of mediocrity, sustained happiness and brief encounters with bliss. Someone asks," Does int it feel good to be in favor of the majority; furthermore, acting in unison with it.? " I reply," Yes, as long as a majority of trees aren't cut down." This seems to be a simple question in response to his question. In advent of climate change I'll work for happiness and devote my energies as a sinister person in the face of rewarding challenge.

It works in accordance with that Americorp's pledge. Trust me, I'm quite "American". Fulfilling the majority responsibility brings about carrying whatever prolonged happiness in affect. It only invites learning in affect to match the gist of prolonged or brief happiness.

"I'll to my best to strengthen communities as a whole. In the face of adversity, I'll persevere., In the face of conflict, I'll seek common ground. As an Americorp's member I'll do my best do get things, in the community. "DONE. (anonymous Americorps member) and conclusion to the story!

IT will be in accordance with service to the government. This, happily is where, I salute, collect my bearings, and leave off-something I didn't cover collectively or solely.

ABOUT THE AUTHOR

Joshua came to reign in the United States of America. Commencing his life in the state of Utah. Obtaining a "fresh start" and means with his original family in Idaho. Experiencing and exploiting the "teenage years" of uncertainty in a remotely subdued niche of New York State. It is claimed the following: chronic mental disabilities are said to come from the "self" or the "environment." As proved, it was the "blank slate" that I naively prospered to become an afflicted adult. Choosing to be a part of the notorious ARMY. Not only this, but by failing to succeed (despite receiving a Bachelor's degree in Psychology) in the exploratory "mecca" of Boston, Massachusetts. My adulthood then had become blemished, wiped out by these two culminating and accumulating experiences. Whereby, claimed and proved to establish a new view on life. This ultimately derives from the usage of medications healing me from the co-existing disorder. What is it said? Tabula-Blank Slate says this: "The environment determines an individual."

www.ingramcontent.com/pod-product-compliance
Lightning Source LLC
Chambersburg PA
CBHW051240120626
46547CB00014B/1724